U0958018

定陵参观导引

A GUIDEBOOK TO THE DINGLING MAUSOLEUM

赵信 编著

學苑出版社

图书在版编目（CIP）数据

定陵参观导引 ：汉英对照 / 赵信编著 . －北京 ：学苑出版社，2010.11

ISBN 978-7-5077-3443-0

Ⅰ . ①定… Ⅱ . ①赵… Ⅲ . ①十三陵－简介－汉、英 Ⅳ . ① K928.76

中国版本图书馆CIP数据核字（2010）第210678号

责任编辑：潘占伟
装帧设计：徐道会
出版发行：学苑出版社
社　　址：北京市丰台区南方庄 2 号院 1 号楼
邮政编码：100079
网　　址：www.book001.com
电子信箱：xueyuan@public.bta.net.cn
销售电话：010-67675512　67678944　67601101（邮购）
经　　销：新华书店
印 刷 厂：保定市彩虹艺雅印刷有限公司
开本尺寸：889×1194　1/32
印　　张：1.25
版　　次：2010 年 11 月第 1 版
印　　次：2010 年 11 月第 1 次印刷
定　　价：5.00 元

目 录
Contents

前 言

《定陵参观导引》是作者参加定陵发掘的真实记录。本书得益于方袁先生的提议，中文经刘勋教授审核；英文由季婧女士翻译，莫润先教授审校。“十三陵帝后陵寝方位图”由中国社会科学院考古研究所李淼、韩慧君教授绘制。

本书的出版得到了定陵博物馆和定陵发掘亲历者庞中威、李树兴、曹国鉴、冼自强等的大力支持。在此，一并致以衷心的感谢！

赵信

2010 年 5 月 1 日

定陵发掘始末及出土文物精品

1955 年 10 月 9 日，秋高气爽，气候宜人。邓小平、李富春、郭沫若、吴晗等国家领导人、专家学者到十三陵游玩。连同工作人员在内，当时约有三四十人。

雄伟壮观的明十三陵掩映于群山绿林之中，别有一番风韵。到达长陵已是中午，所有人都集中到长陵东侧的田野中野餐。人们或坐或站，边吃边谈，很自然地就谈论起十三陵。吴晗作为明史学家、北京市副市长，谈得最多的是长陵。他对郭沫若说："郭老，长陵这么雄伟，陵墓里面也一定很宏大，肯定会有很多珍宝陪葬，说不定还会有很多壁画和绝版古书。咱们把它掘开，搞个地下博物馆，好不好？"郭老表示完全赞同，并对吴晗说："那你就负责起草一份报告给总理，请求批准吧！"

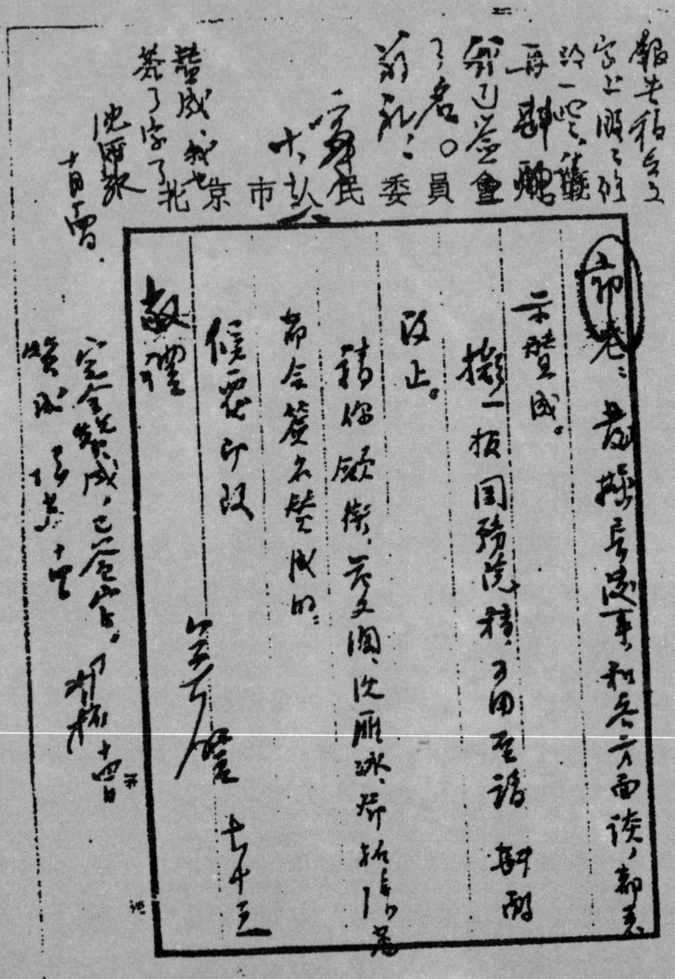

图一 提议发掘长陵的报告

Fig.1 The Report Begging for Approval of the Excavation of the Changling Mausoleum

1955年10月13日，吴晗拟好呈请发掘长陵的报告交给郭沫若审阅，郭沫若做了一些文字上的修改后，与范文澜、沈雁冰、邓拓、张苏一起签字，于10月15日呈送国务院办公厅。10月19日，国务院办公厅呈报周总理，周总理于11月3日批示同意。主管文化工作的陈毅副总理，11月9日也做了相应的批示。自此，发掘长陵的问题就定下来了。总理的决策，揭开了新中国文物考古事业崭新的一页。

既然总理批示的是发掘长陵，为什么后来又发掘了定陵呢？

这是因为帝王陵墓的科学发掘，在中国的历史上是首次，没有经验可资借鉴，而面对的又是祖先丰厚的文化遗产，这神秘的地宫中所埋藏文物的价值是无法估量的。为慎重和保险起见，经周总理同意，决定在正式发掘长陵之前，先试掘一个规模相对较小的陵墓——定陵。

定陵埋葬的是明朝历史上在位时间最长（48年）的万历皇帝——神宗朱翊钧（1563–1620年）。朱翊钧生于嘉靖四十二年(1563年)，隆庆二年（1568年）被册立为皇太子，隆庆六年(1572年)即皇帝位，改元万历。朱翊钧登基时年仅10岁，国事由内阁首辅张居正处理。当时社会矛盾重重，朝廷内部斗争尖锐。张居正力主改革，在他任首辅的10年中，采取了一系列措施，包括整顿吏治、核查田产、疏浚河道、更新税法、抵御海匪等，成效显著。

但是，好景不长。在张居正病死后，顽固派反攻倒算，改

图二 万历皇帝像
Fig.2 Emperor Wanli

革成果付之东流。

朱翊钧成年后，终日沉湎于“酒”、“色”，20年不理朝政，使得吏治空前腐败，百姓处于水深火热之中。此外，他还大兴土木，为自己修建陵墓。定陵的营建在他23岁时就开始了，到28岁才完工，历时5年，每天役使军夫工匠二三万人，总计耗银800万两，致使国库空虚。为满足自己的私欲，他派矿监税使横征暴敛，激起了民众的强烈反抗，给帝国带来深重的灾难。故有“明之亡，实亡于神宗”之说。

试掘定陵的重任最终落到了中国科学院考古研究所和北京市文化局文物组的肩上。由于这是一项意义重大而带有紧迫性的工作，双方及时抽调工作人员组成发掘队，由著名考古学家夏鼐主持。作为考古所的成员，我们几个年轻人有幸参加了发掘工作。

1956年5月17日，定陵发掘工作正式开始。

考古工作者们是第一次发掘皇陵，谁也不知道地宫的大门在什么位置。在这种情况下，为了找到陵墓隧道的准确位置，就在明楼后面，挖了一条长50米宽3米的探沟。此后工作进展缓慢。1957年三四月份，在探沟里挖出了一块小石碑，石碑上书：“此石至金刚墙前皮十六丈深三丈五尺”。指路小石碑的出现，引起了大家的争论，有的说，这是一块迷路碑，皇帝故意埋下的；有的说是大臣搞的鬼……最终大家取得一致看

图三 指路小石碑
Fig.3 The Small Stone Tablet

法，认为从小石碑记载的详细数据来看，这可能是皇帝死后下葬时进入地宫的标记。寿宫建好后，隧道要用土填埋。帝后一旦去世，隧道要及时开掘，所以工匠留下记号，便于日后工作。正因为如此，石碑的出现，被考古人员喻为打开地宫大门的一把钥匙。此后挖掘的进度加快了。

随着发掘的进展，各种各样的传说和议论也慢慢多了起来：有的说地宫里面有毒气，一不小心就会中毒身亡；有的说下面设有翻板，人要踏上去就会掉进陷阱，里面埋了一排排的尖刀；有的说里面预先设置了强弓弩箭，能把人乱箭射死；有的说上面有千斤石，人一触动机关，就会被砸成肉饼。在这样的氛围下，长陵祾恩殿又发生了雷劈死人的事件。 那是1957年8月的一天，雷电交加，大雨倾盆。在长陵祾恩殿，一声炸雷，劈死了一个在此避雨的村民。传说和现实发生的事情，更增加了工作人员心理上的恐惧和不安。

1957年9月中旬，陵道里的填土全部清理完毕。一道大明砖砌起的金刚墙横在陵道的尽头。金刚墙是以巨大条石为基，石基上面以青砖垒砌，高达四五十层。金刚墙的中央，是一个“圭”形的门。由于陵道填土多年的侧压力，“圭”形门上的砌砖向里凹进去约有2厘米。“圭”形门上的砌砖没有用灰浆填缝，是干垒起来的，不是人们猜测的用铜水浇铸的金刚墙。考古工作者百感交集，知道进入地宫为时不远了。

9月17日，拆除金刚墙“圭”形门的工作开始了，民工在“圭”形门上端拆开了一个洞。随着明砖的拆除，墓室里的

图四 金刚墙及“圭”形门
Fig.4 “圭”— Shaped Gate in the Diamond Wall

腐朽气体飘了出来，使现场的人员难以忍受。再加上先前的传说，人们真的相信墓室里有毒气。考古技佐白万玉决定先散散墓室里的气味，第二天再继续工作。

第二天上午，所有的考古人员都等待着一个特殊时刻的到来。之前我们买了一条狗，准备投进去先探探路。怎奈在昭陵村买的狗太凶猛，把去牵狗的人吓得跑了回来。考虑到如果真把狗放进去，会把里面的东西碰坏，于是放狗进去一事就做罢了。大家又想到放一只鸡进去试试看。考古人员拎着一只鸡攀上梯子，用力从打开的黑洞抛了进去。惊恐的鸡“嘎嘎嘎”地叫着从洞口飞了出来，跑掉了。两次试验全部失败，白万玉心事重重，一言不发。大家心里明白，此时，只有找人从洞口下去一探究竟了。

到了下午，大家都聚到了金刚墙前。“圭”形门上黑幽幽的洞口，犹如猛兽张开的大口，正静静地等待着送到嘴里的猎物……白万玉扫视了一下现场的人，最终把饱含期待的目光落在了他徒弟庞中威的身上，命令他第一个下去探路。

当第一个下定陵的人确定为庞中威之后，所有的准备工作就有条不紊地展开了，大家备齐各种工具，包括汽灯、麻绳、手电、梯子、安全帽等等。下午四五点钟，从金刚墙上 3 米处拆开的洞口，先放进去一个竹梯，靠在金刚墙的内壁上。金刚墙的外面，靠了两个梯子。庞中威的腰部被麻绳捆住，他背着手电筒顺梯而下。外面有人拽着绳子。其他人都蹲在洞口，用手电照着。为了他的安全，我让他戴上安全帽。他却说：“柳条帽没用，石条一翻，钢盔也能砸扁，不用戴了。”庞中威在他写的《定陵发掘亲历记》一书中对其当时的心情有一段描述：“就是在这紧张的气氛中，我一步一步下到地宫隧道的地面上。在围着地宫隧道走了两圈之后，看没有什么的危险，就向洞口喊道：‘下来个人吧！别担心了。我踩过了，全踩过了。没事了，洞口的赵先生下来吧！’过了约有 10 分钟，赵其昌也顺着梯子下到地宫里。遂道尽头是一座石门，我们两个人就

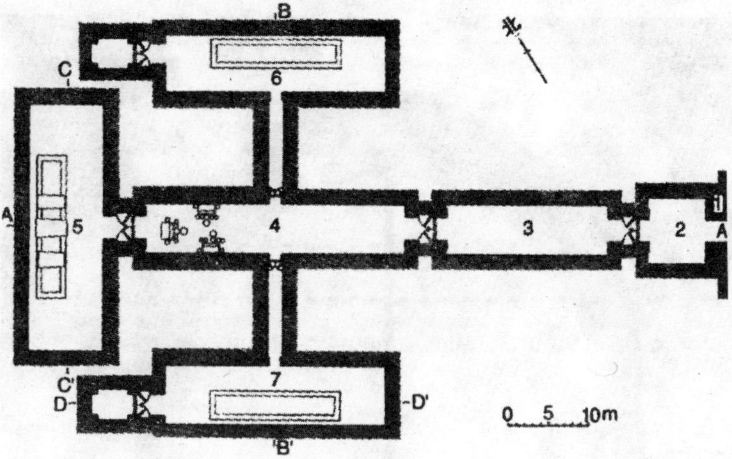

图五 定陵地官平面图
Fig.5 Plan of the Crypt

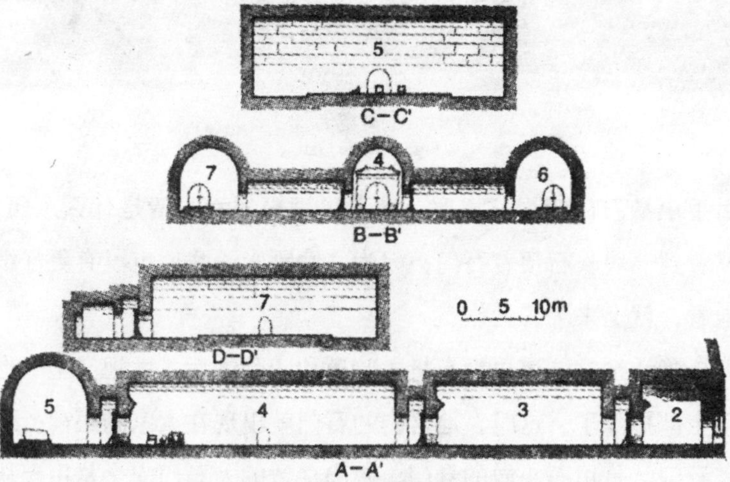

图六 定陵地官剖面图
Fig.6 Section of the Crypt

图七 定陵地宫石门
Fig.7 Stone Gate

用手电从石门缝里往里照，地下黑糊糊的看不清是什么东西，只看到一块长石顶着石门。因为心情紧张，我们也没有更仔细地看，就上来了。”

确认地宫隧道里没有机关暗道和凶险之后，就把“圭”形门全部拆除了。这时，地宫内的石门就出现在大家的眼前。地宫石门，是用石头做的券门。两扇精致的大石门完全是用整块汉白玉做成，洁白光润，晶莹夺目。每扇门重达 7 吨左右，门上刻了纵横各9排门钉，还雕有兽首衔环，格外壮丽。石门是紧闭的,从门缝里看进去,被一个石条顶着,从外面是推不开的。

石门是如何打开的呢？

9月19日下午，所有的工作人员都聚到了地宫的石门前。白万玉手里拿着一根带弯的铁丝，铁丝一头栓着绳子。木工带着刮好的几根竹板。所有的人都好奇，凭这点东西能打开14吨重的石门吗？白万玉先让把铁丝弯个半圆，立着从门缝里插进去，再转过来，套住顶门石的腰部，然后把外面多余的铁丝边弯边往里送，慢慢地铁丝的头回转过来，形成了一个完整的铁丝圈，再把铁丝圈拧死，这样就做成了一个套牢顶门石的圈。几个人控制着铁丝圈，防止顶门石倒下摔坏，其他人用竹板顶着顶门石的上端，用力去推。在大家努力下，顶门石慢慢离开石门。几次反复，门被推开有两尺多宽了。这时进去一人，移开了顶门石。关闭了300多年的地宫大门，终于在沉重的嗡嗡声中徐徐敞开了。地宫的全貌完全呈现在大家的眼前。地宫由5个极其高大宽敞的殿堂联结而成，全为拱券石结构，没有一根梁柱。前殿、中殿、后殿联结起来，形成一个“丁”形甬道，两侧还有左右配殿。整个地宫里共有7道门，只有前殿的石门是关着的。

石门打开后，大家进入地宫前殿。地面上铺着木板，均已腐朽，木板下墁铺着金砖。所谓金砖，并不是用金子做的砖，而是明朝宫廷特地在江南烧造的方砖，专用铺地。制造这种砖有“澄浆”一道工序，因此又叫“澄浆砖”。又因质地细腻，

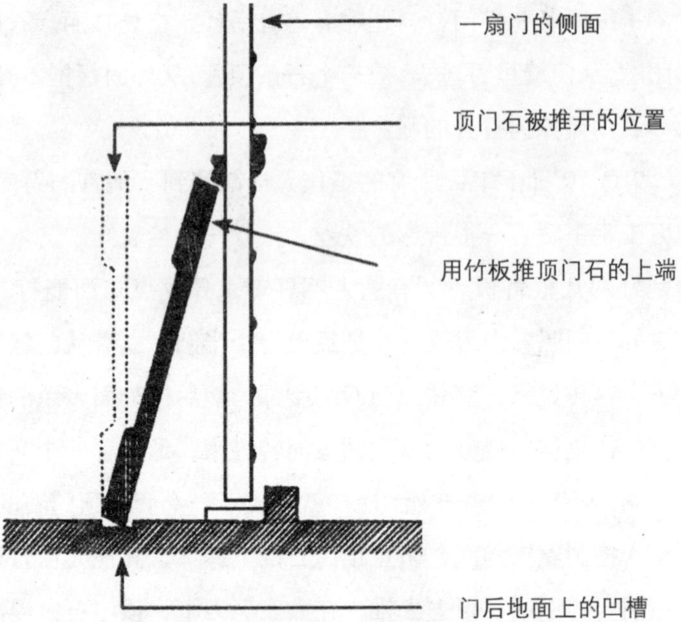

图八 打开地宫石门示意图
Fig.8 Schematic Drawing of Opening the Stone Gate

图九 前殿铺地木板
Fig.9 The Wood Paved on the Floor of the Anterior Hall

扣之有金石之声，所以又称“金砖”。从前殿走进中殿，在中殿的后部，放着石宝座。石宝座上面铺有锦丝垫，已经腐烂了。还有五供桌、蜡烛等。蜡烛已变形弯曲，红色，上有蟠龙纹浮雕。此外还有万年灯。所谓万年灯，就是一个装满香油高约 70 厘米的大青花瓷缸。但从现场看，万年灯没有点过，缸里的油呈黑色，已经凝固了。缸的中间有一根小手指粗细的铜管露出缸口，一个用布缠着的圆圈，串在铜管上，浮在已凝固的油面上，上面露出 3 个灯捻。

中殿两侧是左配殿和右配殿。两个配殿的棺床上空无一物。在棺床中央，都留有一个长 0.4 米宽 0.2 米的方孔，里面填满黄土。这是个风水穴，叫做“金井”，用以沟通阴阳两界。

图十 地宫中殿陈设
Fig.10 Original View of the Middle Hall of the Crypt

入葬后，棺椁必须端端正正地压在金井之上，以接地气。与自然融为一体，死者的灵魂才能永世长存，家族才能万世兴旺……就是出于这种宗教思想，历代皇陵在寿宫营建之初，开工的第一撮土都要妥善地保存起来，等地宫建成后，再把它极其郑重地填入金井之中。

看完中殿和左右配殿后，就进入后殿了，也就是皇帝和皇后的寝宫。棺床上停放着3口红色棺椁，中间是万历皇帝的，左边是孝端皇后的，右边是孝靖皇后的。棺材用楠木做成，外涂朱漆。棺材板已腐烂。棺外为木椁，椁底板上镶嵌四个大铜环。棺椁周围，放着很多大块玉料。棺床上放置不少木箱，杂乱无序。木箱上拴的绳子没有打结，木箱的抬杠也没有抽掉。长时间的潮湿使箱子已多半腐朽，箱内的东西滚落在外。有镶满珠玉的盔甲和宝剑，以及金银器皿、谥册、宝印、木马、木俑、精致的凤冠、小巧的房屋模型……横七竖八。从现场一片狼籍的迹象看来，当时的入葬比较慌乱。

地宫完全打开之后两个多月，开始着手清理棺椁。在3口棺椁中，右侧是孝靖皇后王氏的。孝靖皇后比万历皇帝早死10年，先埋在东井左侧的平冈地，后来由她的孙子朱由校将其棺椁迁出，移放定陵，故损坏较为严重。孝靖皇后原是万历皇帝母亲孝定皇后的侍女，一次偶然的机会，万历皇帝临幸了王氏。后来王氏生下光宗皇帝，但万历皇帝并不喜欢王氏母子。由于万历皇帝一直宠爱郑贵妃，故孝靖始终被冷落宫中。王氏死后，万历皇帝并不把她的丧事放在心上，仅谥为“温肃端静

图十一 地宫后殿原貌
Fig.11 Original View of the Rear Hall of the Crypt

纯懿皇贵妃”，其他则一概不问。孝靖儿子光宗登极，下诏追谥母亲为皇太后，但礼仪未行，自己先崩。孙子熹宗登极，又尊王氏为“孝靖温懿敬让贞慈参天胤圣皇太后”，并迁葬定陵，与万历皇帝合葬。

孝靖皇后的棺木打开之后，一床残存“南无阿弥……”字样的鹅黄色织锦经被显现在大家面前。锦被之下塞满了金、银、玉等殉葬品。还有两套精美鲜艳的服装，上衣是黄缎夹袄，下身则是黄缎裙。这是定陵出土的最为珍贵而且也是保存最好的两件价值连城的瑰宝。

随葬衣物中有一件绣着100个童子的上衣夹袄，织锦精致，童子组成40个画面，如“考试图”、“官员出行图”、“捕鸟图”、“打猫图”、“捉迷藏图”、“摘鲜桃图”、“放爆竹图 ”、“沐浴图”、“跳绳图”等，儿童神态迥异，个个活灵活现，生动逼真。

图十二　百子衣复原图
Fig.12 Reconstructed Jacket with One Hundred Children Design

百子衣上除织绘出动植物花纹图案外，尚有一个神秘的“卐”字形符号。“卐”音读“万”，唐玄奘将其译为“德”字。该符号具有强烈而浓厚的宗教气氛，是在大唐帝国时，由波斯、印度和我国西藏等地传入内地的。

孝靖皇后的尸体，只残存一副骨架，为侧卧式：左臂下垂，手放在腰部；右臂向上弯屈，手放在头部附近；下肢伸直。头枕在织锦枕面上。头上插满金、玉、宝石钗簪，身下铺满了纸钱与铜钱。

万历皇帝棺椁的左侧，置放着他的原配孝端皇后王氏的棺椁，也是香楠木制成。椁棺具全。打开木棺，里面有一床绣有九龙纹饰的织锦被及殉葬的漆盒，金器衣物等。骨架完好，头西脚东，左臂下垂，手放在腰部，右臂伸直；下肢相叠压，左脚在上，右脚在下。头枕一个长方形锦制枕头，发绺上插满了镶有宝石的金簪。在尸骨的下面，铺有一床缀着100枚金钱的褥子，金钱上铸有“消灾延寿”字样。褥子两侧，放置了大量

图十三 孝端皇后像
Fig.13 Empress Xiaoduan

图十四 孝靖皇后像
Fig.14 Empress Xiaojing

的金元宝，元宝两面都刻有填朱文字。

万历皇帝的棺椁，亦为楠木制成，棺木上面铺盖着黄色丝织铭旗，两端镶木制龙牌。铭旗中央金书“大行皇帝梓宫”六个大字。棺内装满了珍宝。锦被下面露出形色各异的道袍、龙袍等。下层，有稀世瑰宝一件，就是万历皇帝的缂丝十二团龙十二章衮服龙袍。衮服是龙袍中的精品，是皇帝在祭拜和举行大典时所穿的礼服。

打开对折的锦被，露出躺在锦被之上的万历皇帝尸骨。已是一具骷髅头西脚东，左臂下垂，手放在腹部，攥着一串佛珠。右臂向上弯屈，手放在下颏附近。嘴边有一缕黄褐色胡须。脊柱上部略弯曲，左腿伸直，右腿微屈，脚向外撇。身着龙袍，

图十五 翼善金冠
Fig.15 Gold Crown

图十六 缂丝二团龙十二章衮服龙袍复原图
Fig.16 Kesi Tapestry Dragon Robe with 12 Dragon Roundels

腰束一条玉带，头戴“翼善冠”。棺内放置着一层排列有序而多达69匹的织锦。头骨的右侧，放着一个圆形盒子。盒内居然是一顶金光灿烂、极为富丽的翼善金冠。这顶金冠，全部用极为精细的金丝编织而成，重826克。弧形的帽山上竖立着两片金丝网片，如太阳似的明飘悬在两网片之间，两条金黄色的游龙爪踏帽山，举首仰望明珠，栩栩如生，不愧为世之瑰宝。

清理完棺椁，考古工作者发现了一箱用檀香木板制成的谥册。谥册的文字，概括总结了万历皇帝的一生功绩。

定陵地宫打开后，消息不胫而走。当时出土的尸骨、文物还没有清理，博物馆也未建立，但各界人士都想前来先睹为快。当时前来定陵参观者有朱德、宋庆龄、彭德怀、贺龙、刘伯承、李济深、郭沫若、林枫、廖承志、杨成武、许广平、邓拓、郑振铎、王冶秋、王昆仑、齐燕铭、杨勇和王平等人。

1959年9月，定陵博物馆正式对公众开放。展品以地宫出土文物为主，配以地下宫殿的发掘照片、图表模型等，计展出文物233件（套），分为金器、瓷器、丝织品、锡冥器以及帝后的冠带、首饰等类。定陵玄宫的陈列基本保持发掘时的原貌。出土文物陈列，后来设于长陵祾恩殿内。1985年4月，定陵博物馆对外宾开放，陈列面积1200平方米，展品为定陵部分出土文物及复制品，计195件（套）。如今，定陵地宫开放已40多年，大凡到北京的中外游客，没有不去定陵的。定陵以它那恢宏的气势迎接着四面八方的来客。

附录　十三陵皇帝简表

陵名	年号	庙号	名字	即位时间	即位年龄	在位年数	死亡时间	死时年龄	世系
长陵	永乐	成祖	朱　棣	建文四年（1402）	43	42	永乐二十二年（1424）	65	朱元璋之第四子
献陵	洪熙	仁宗	朱高炽	永乐二十二年（1424）	47	1	洪熙元年（1425）	48	朱棣之长子
景陵	宣德	宣宗	朱瞻基	洪熙元年（1425）	28	10	宣德十年（1435）	38	朱高炽之长子
裕陵	正统	英宗	朱祁镇	宣德十年（1435）	9	14	正统十四年被俘		朱瞻基之长子
茂陵	成化	宪宗	朱见深	天顺八年（1464）	18	23	成化二十三年（1487）	41	朱祁镇之长子
泰陵	弘治	孝宗	朱祐樘	成化二十三年（1487）	18	18	弘治十八年（1505）	36	朱见深之第三子
康陵	正德	武宗	朱厚照	弘治十八年（1505）	15	16	正德十六年（1521）	31	朱祐樘之长子
永陵	嘉靖	世宗	朱厚熜	正德十六年（1521）	15	45	嘉靖四十五年（1567）	60	朱祐樘之侄
昭陵	隆庆	穆宗	朱载垕	嘉靖四十五年（1567）	30	6	隆庆六年（1572）	36	朱厚熜之第三子
定陵	万历	神宗	朱翊钧	隆庆六年（1572）	10	48	万历四十八年（1620）	58	朱载垕之第三子
庆陵	泰昌	光宗	朱常洛	万历四十八年（1620）	39	30 天	泰昌元年（1620）	39	朱翊钧之长子
德陵	天启	熹宗	朱由校	泰昌元年（1620）	16	7	天启七年（1627）	23	朱常洛之长子
思陵	崇祯	思宗	朱由俭	天启七年（1627）	18	17	崇祯十七年	35	朱常洛之第五子

Preface

The Guidebook to the Dingling Mausoleum is a true record of mine on my participation in the excavation of the tomb. It must be of benefit to read the story.

This booklet is written on Mr. Fang Yuan's suggestion. Prof. Liu Xun edited the Chinese text, Miss Ji Jing translated it into English, Prof. Mo Runxian revised the English version, and Profs. Li Miao and Han Huijun drew the map of the Ming tombs.

The publication of the book is thanks to support from the Dingling Mausoleum Museum, as well as people involved the excavation of the DingLing Mausoleum, Pang Zhongwei, Li Shuxing, Cao Guojian, Xian Ziqiang.

To all of the above personages I would like to express my gratitude and appreciation.

Zhao Xin

1st May 2010

Story of the Excavation of the Dingling Mausoleum and Select Cultural Relics from the Tomb

It was a fine, delightful autumn day in October 1955. Deng Xiaoping, Li Fuchun and Guo Moruo, leaders of PRC and scholars visited the Ming Tombs. Along with them were Prof. Wu Han and about thirty to forty workers.

The magnificent Ming Tombs emerged amongst picturesque hills and trees. It was already midday when Deng Xiaoping and the others arrived at the Changling Mausoleum. Then all of them gathered to have a picnic in a spot east of the tomb, some sitting and others standing. While having the dinner, they talked, naturally, about the Ming Tombs. As a historian on the Ming Dynasty and a Vice Mayor of Beijing City, Wu Han talked mostly about the Changling Mausoleum. He said to Guo Morou: "Reverend Guo, the Changling is so great and its interior must be also magnificent. There must be a lot of treasures as funeral objects. Perhaps it has many murals and old books unavailable elsewhere. What about our excavating the tomb and building an underground museum?" Prof. Guo absolutely agreed with that and said to Wu: "You should write a report to the Premier to apply for approval."

On 13th Oct.1955, Wu Han drew up the report and presented it to Guo Moruo to process. Guo examined the draft and made some literal revision. Then he put down his signature on the document along with the veteran scholars Fan Wenlan, Shen Yanbing, Deng Tuo and Zhang Su. On 15th Oct., the report was presented to the General Office of the State Council. On 19th, it was submitted to Premier Zhou, who approved it on 3rd Nov.; after that, Vice-premier Chen Yi in charge of national cultural affairs had made similar comments on 9th Nov. Thus the matter of excavating the Changling Mausoleum was decided. The Premier's crucial decision opened a new chapter in the history of the New China's cultural and archaeological undertakings. (See p.3/Fig.1)

Now that the Premier approved the excavation of Changling, why was the Dingling Mausoleum to be excavated later?

It was because this was the first time that an imperial mausoleum had been scientifically excavated in the history of China, there was no experience for reference, and what the mysterious tomb contains is a great batch of invaluable cultural relics our ancestors left us. For the sake of caution, with the Premier's permission, it was decided to excavate the Dingling, a relatively small tomb on scale, as an object of trial before digging the Changling.

The tomb-owner of Dingling is the Ming Emperor Zhu Yijun (1563—1620), or Wanli by reign title and Shenzong by temple title, whose reign lasted for 48 years. He was born in the 42nd year of Jiajing reign (1563) and titled Crown Prince in the 2nd Longqing year (1568). At the age of ten, in the 6th Longqing year (1572), he came to the throne and changed the reign title into "Wanli". As he was too little for an actual ruler, the national administrative affairs were shifted over to Grand Cabinet Academician Zhang Juzheng. It was an age full of contradictions in society and conflicts in the imperial government. Zhang carried out energetically a series of reforms: for ten years he rectified officials' administration, examined landed property, dredged water-ways, innovated tax regulations, fought against seabandit gangs, and so on. All these got great achievements and demons-trated the might and dignity of the Ming Empire. (See p.4/Fig.2)

But the good times did not last long. After Zhang died of illness, the diehards madea counterattack, and the reform accomplishments were abolished.

Zhu Yijin grew up into a man indulging in wine and feminine charms. For 20 years he paid no attention to state administration. It made officials seriously corrupt and thc common people live in deep distress. But Zhu closed his eyes to the situation; moreover, he launched an immense construction project to build his mausoleum on large amounts of flesh and blood of the people. The works were begun at his age of 23 and completed when he was 28 years old, lasting five years. It required daily 20,000 to 30,000 laborers from armed forces and the common people, and cost 8,000,000 taels of silver in total. As a result, the state treasury was severely depleted, officials extorted excessive taxes and levies, and the empire wasfaced with a great calamity. It aroused the populace to resistance. Historians remarked: "The fall of the Ming was actually due to Shenzong."

The burden of the trial excavation of Dingling was put on the shoulders of the Institute of Archaeology under the Chinese Academy of Sciences and the Section of Cultural Relics under the Beijing Municipal Bureau of Culture. Realizing the urgency and importance of the task, the two institutions immediately organized an excavating team with the famous archaeologist Xia Nai as the director. As members of the Institute, some young people, me included, had the good fortune to join the team.

On 17th May 1956, the excavation of Dingling was formally started.

This was the first time the excavators had been confronted with an imperial mausoleum; we did not know where the gate of the underground palace was. To find out the exact location of the tomb tunnel, we dug a 50m long, 3m wide trench extending from behind the Minglou Memorial Tower. After over 300-dayimplementation of the established plan, a small stone tablet was found bearing the inscription "It is 16 zhang(about 53.3m) long from here to the frontal surface of the diamond wall with a depth of 3.5 zhang (approximately 11.7m)." The emergence of the guidepost aroused a debate among the teamfellows: some saying this must have been a confusing stone buried by the imperial's order, others believing it to have been senior officials' trick...... Finally we came to the unanimous opinion that, in the light of the detailed datum on the tablet, this was very likely a mark for the convenience of entombing the late emperor into the underground palace. After the completion of the crypt, the tunnel was to be filled with earth; once the emperor and his empresses died, it would be opened in time. It was just for this reason that the stone tablet was likened to a key for opening the gate of the underground palace. From then on, the work was accelerated. (See p.5/Fig.3)

As the excavation went on, various rumors and gossips arose one after another. One of them asserted that there were poison gases inside, which would kill the careless enterers; another said that there was a murdering device and once you stepped on it, you would fall into a trap and be killed by pointed knives in rows, crossbows-and-arrows or stones weighting thousands of kilograms. Meanwhile, realities were also a big threat to us. For example, on a downpour day in Aug. 1957, a villager, while taking shelter from the rain in the Ling'en Hall of Changling Mausoleum, was killed by lighting.

In mid Sep. 1957, the soil in the tunnel was cleared away. A brick structure, i.e. the diamond wall, emerged at the end of the tunnel. It has a foundation built of long, narrow huge stones and a body of livid bricks in 40—50 courses. In the middle is a " 圭 "-shaped gate, the brick barrier of which has been caved inward for about 2cm due to the longtime sidewise pressure of the soil in the tunnel. It is built up without any mortar, nor with the liquid copper as people guessed. Realizing soon it would be the time to enter the underground palace, we got extremely excited and all sorts of feelings arose in our mind. (See p.7/Fig.4)

On 17th Sep. the brick filling of the doorway began to be torn down, and a hole was soon made in its upper part. Along with the removal of the bricks, a smell of decay came out from the tomb-chamber, producing an atmosphere terrible to all present. It seemed that the saying of poison gases in the crypt was believable. Then Bai Wanyu, a veteran archaeological technician from our Institute, decided to stop the work until the smell escaped thoroughly the next day.

The next morning, we all were waiting for the coming of the especial moment. At first we planned to put a dog into the tomb to feel out the danger there. But the dog bought from Zhaoling Village was so ferocious that its guide was threatened and ran away. Moreover, a dog let in would damage whatever it ran into. So this plan was abandoned. Then another idea was begun to try, i.e. putting a chicken in. Someone climbs up the ladder with the chicken in hand and throws it into the tomb. But the chicken was frightened, flied out with piercing cry, and ran away. Thus both the experiments failed. Bai Wanyu became speechless with a heavy heart, while the others dared not ask him for means, as we all were unhappy at the situation. It was obviously that the only way was letting somebody get in. (See p.9/Fig.5, Fig.6)

In the afternoon we gathered again at the diamond wall, feeling anxious about the way out. The dark hole in the wall looks like a beast's wideopened frightful mouth, as if waiting quietly for its preys. Bai takes a glance at his fellow present, while the latter stare at his serious face. Finally he casts his expectant eyes upon his apprentice Pang Zhongwei and asks Pang to shoulder the pioneering mission.

All preparations were begun soon after Pang was appointed. Tools, gas lamps, ropes, flashlights, ladders, safety helmets and so on were gathered on the site. At four to five o'clock p.m., a bamboo ladder was put into the crypt through the hole 3m above the tunnel bottom and leaned against the inner wall surface, and two ladders were furnished against the outer side. Pang goes to the bamboo ladder, flashlight hanging at his back, rope tied round the waist with the lower end in the hand of his team-fellows squatting by the hole and illuminating his way with flashlights. For his safety I put a helmet on his head, but he says:"The wicker cap has no use. Even a steel helmet will be flattened when a stone falls down from the top. I needn't it." In his recently published work Dingling Mausoleum: a Personal Experience of Its Excavation he describes the then frame of his mind:"In the tense atmosphere I go down step by step toward the floor of the tunnel. After walking round in two circles inside and making sure of no danger there, I shout to the hole: 'Please someone come down here! Don't worry. I've tried it, tried over all. Surely here is no danger. Please Mr. Zhao come down through the hole.'About ten minutes later, Zhao Qichang climbed down the ladder, too. At the end of the tunnel is a stone gate. We light up the inside through the door gap with our flashlights. In the darkness anything can't be clearly seen except for a long stone propping the door-leaves.Full of a tense mood, we get out in a hurry, taking no careful look at the interior."

The condition was proved safe. There were neither hidden weapons nor other ferocious danger, so the " 圭 "-shaped door-barrier was completely removed. Now the stone gate of the underground palace was clearly revealed before us. Under a stone arch are two white marble door-leaves made of whole blocks, bright and clean, each weighting about 7t and bearing nine vertical and horizontal rows of nipples and a sculptured knocker in the shape of an animal holding a ring in the mouth, which add great magnificence to the building. The door was tightly closed and could not be pushed open from outside as the door-leaves were heavily pressed inside with a huge natural stone. (See p.10/Fig.7)

How did the stone gate get opened?

On 19th Sep., in the afternoon, all the workers gathered in front of the stone gate. Bai Wanyu was holding an iron wire with a curve made at one end and a rope tied on the other, and the woodworker, scraped long bamboo bars. We were surprised to see the scene:Can the 14t door-leaves be opened with these tools? The woodworker operated under Bai's direction while the others were looking on. A section of the wire is first bent into a semi-circle, which is vertically inserted into the door gap, turned to a horizontal position, and thus hooked onto the middle of the door-propping stone. Then the rest of the wine is also made bent and inserted in to make the semi-circular section of the wire come back gradually and form a complete circle. The ends of the circle are joined and screwed up to tie up the propping stone. Now some people control the wirecircle to prevent the propping stone from falling and breaking, while others prop up and push the top of the stone with the bamboo bars. Little by little the stone gets off its position and the door-leaves are gradually opened until the door gap is widened for over 60cm. Then someone enters the tomb and removes the stone away. Thus the crypt gate closed more than 300 years eventually got opened in a low hum, and the full view of the underground palace appeared before us. The building consists of five high, spacious halls under stone vaults with neither pillars nor beams. Among them the anterior, middle and rear halls are laid out in a T-shaped plan, and the two auxiliary halls are arranged on the sides of the middle hall. Altogether there are seven stone doorways in the underground palace, of which only that of the anterior hall was closed. (See p.12/ Fig.8)

After the stone gate got opened, all people present entered the anterior hall. Here the floor is paved with wood, which, unfortunately, has rotten away. Beneath this pavement is a layer of so-called "golden brick" square in plan, produced in South China exclusively for floor pavement in the Ming palace. One of its making processes was clay precipitating, so it was also called precipitated-clay brick. The name "golden brick" was given for its fineness in texture and for its properties of producing a metal-like sound when being stricken. Walking in the middle hall, we saw at the back rotten silk covered stone thrones, sacrificial vessels and candlesticks. The candles are red, have become curved and are decorated with dragon designs in relief. The rest of objects include"everburning lamps", i.e. a blue-and-white porcelain vat filled with sesame oil. They seem not to have been lit, and the oil has become black and solid. From the center a little-finger-thin copper tube is stretched outward and revealed at the vessel rim, and three lamp-wicks are stuck out of the surface of the so-lidified oil from the ring tied up onto the tube with a ribbon. (See p.12/Fig.9)

The two auxiliary halls are furnished with a coffin platform each. But nothing has been found on the structure except for a loess-filled 0.4m long, 0.2m wide hole at the center, a geomantic pit intended to communicate this world with the nether one. According to the relevant institution, the coffin, when entombed, was to be placed in the position with its center right on this "golden well" so as to be joined with the earth. The intention was to make the soul of the tomb-owner merged with the nature and living forever and to ensure his family everlasting prosperity. Just out of this religious thought, ancient dynasties observed the practice that pinches of earth would be gathered from the burial ground when an imperial mausoleum began to be built, and kept until being solemnly put into the "golden well" after the completion of the underground palace. (See p.13/Fig.10)

After watching the middle hall and the side ones, we arrived at the rear hall, the burial chamber of the emperor and his wives. On the coffin-platform are three red coffins with that of the Emperor Wanli flanked by those of the Empresses Xiaoduan and Xiaojing on the left and right respectively. They are made of nanmu wood and painted in red lacquer on the surface, all in decay. The outer coffin bears four large copper rings inlaid on the bottom plank and is surrounded with blocks of jade material, beside which are a lot of wooden cases in jumble, with the ropes unknotted but still kept on them, and the stout poles have not been taken away. Owing to the moisture in the crypt, the cases have largely rotten away, and the objects inside have been scattered out. Among these are jade-and jewel-inlaid helmets, armor plates and swords, gold and silver wares, wooden tablets with inscriptions on posthumous title giving, seals, wooden horses and tomb-figurines, exquisite phoenix coronets and fine model houses, all in disorderly heaps. It suggests that the entombment must have been in a rush. (See p.15/Fig.11)

Two months after the entirely opening of the underground palace, we started to clear out the coffins. Of them the right one is that of the Empress Xiaojing surnamed Wang. Dying ten years earlier than Wanli's death, she was first buried on a tableland on the left side of Dongjing, so her coffin rotted sooner. Later, it was removed into the Dingling Mausoleum by her grandson Zhu Youxiao, which caused a still greater damage. Before her death, she was originally one of the maids of the Empress Xiaoding, the Emperor Wanli's mother. Once she got a chance favor from Wanli, and then gave birth to the future emperor Guangzong. But Wanli did not like Wang and her son; his constant love to his concubine Lady Zheng made Wang left out in the cold all along. Even to her death he showed little concern except for granting her the posthumous title "Highest-ranking Imperial Concubine". After ascending the throne, her son Guangzong conferred her the title "Empress Dowager". But he died before conducting the relevant ceremony. Then her grandson Xizong ascended the throne. He added a series of honorific words to this title, and removed her coffin into the Dingling Mausoleum, making her corpse joinWanli's.

Opening Empress Xiaojing's coffin, we saw the remains of a yellow brocade quilt with a Buddhist inscription eulogizing Amitabha. Beneath it are numerous gold, silver and jade funeral objects, as well as two lady'suits, exquisite in workmanship and bright in color, either consisting of a lined yellow-satin jacket and a skirt of the same fabric. These are the most valuable and the best-preserved treasures from the tomb.

One of the jackets is embroidered with one hundred children in 40 scenes, which represent taking an examination, official's procession, catching birds, playing with cats, playing hide-and-seek, gathering peaches,letting off firecrackers, bathing, skipping ropes, and so on. The figures are different from each other in appearance and expression, all portrayed truly and vividly. (See p.16/Fig.12)

In addition to faunal and floral designs, among the motifs is a mysterious "卍"-shaped sign, which should be pronounced "wan" and translated into the character "de 德 " (virtue) as the Tang eminent monk Xuanzang deciphered. It shows a strong religious trait and must have been introduced into China's hinterland from Persia, India and China's Tibet in the Tang period.

Of the Empress Xiaojing's corpse only the skeleton remains. It lies sideward, left arm stretched along body, hand at waist; right arm bent up-ward, hand beside head; and lower limbs straightened. The head rests on a brocade pillow, with gold, jade and jewel hairpins remaining in situ. Beneath the body are layers of paper and copper coins. (See p.17/Fig.14)

On the left of Wanli's coffin stands that of his first wife Wang by surname and Xiaoduan by posthumous title, which is also a double nanmu-wood coffin. The funeral objects it contains include a brocade quilt embroidered with nine-dragon design, as well as lacquered caskets, gold ware and clothes. The skeleton is in a good condition, head pointing to the west and feet to the east; left arm stretched along body, hand at waist; right arm straightened; lower limbs crossed with left foot on right one; head on a rectangular brocade pillow, hair covered with jewel-inlaid gold headgears. Beneath the skeleton is a cotton-padded mattress decorated with one hundred gold coins, which are cast with the inscription "xiao zai yan shou 消灾延寿" (happiness and longevity). It is flanked by numbers of shoe-shaped gold ingots with red-filled characters in intaglio on both sides. (See p.17/Fig.13)

The coffin of the Emperor Wanli is made of nanmu, too. Its top is covered with a yellow silkflag bearing the gold inscription "Daxing Huangdi Zigong 大行皇帝梓宫" (Coffin of the Grand Emperor) in the middle, and the boards are inlaid with wooden dragon plaques. The interior is full of treasures. Various clothes, such as Taoist coats and dragon robes, are revealed from beneath a brocade quilt. In the bottom layer is an extremely valuable dragon robe of kesi tapestry with 12 dragon roundels, a finest work of art among the dragon robes. It is the emperor's formal attire, in which he conducted national sacrificial rites and other grand ceremonies. (See p.18/Fig.16)

Opening the brocade quilt folded in two, we saw the Emperor Wanli's skeleton. It lies in a supine position, head pointing to the west while feet to the east; left arm stretched along body, hand on belly, holding a Buddhist rosary; right arm bent upward, hand beside mandible; and a lock of yellowish-brown beard kept near mouth. The spinal column is slightly crooked in the upper section; the left leg is straightened, while the right one, some-what bent; and the feet incline outward. The dress on the skeleton includs a dragon robe on the body, a jade belt at the waist, and a crown on the head; and brocade rolls, totaling as many as 69 bolts, are neatly laid in the coffin. On the right of the head is a round box, in which a gold crown remains resplendent. It is all knitted of very fine gold wire, weighting 826g. On the arched top, two pieces of gold-wire net are erected in the flanks. In the middle of them, a pearl, which looks like the sun rising in the air, and double golden dragons ascend up the top, head raised to watch the pearl. Vivid in representation, it is really a worldwide rare gem.(See p.18/Fig.15)

While the coffin was clearing, a case was discovered containing a batch of sandalwood tablets with an inscription on the emperor's post-humous title giving. The text sums up Wanli's merits and achievements in his whole life.

As soon as the underground palace of Dingling was opened, the news was spread like wildfire. People from all walks of life desired to watch the findings, considering it a pleasure to be among the first visitors, although the unearthed human remains and cultural relics had not been sifted and the museum had not been set up yet. Soon there came Zhu De, Song Qingling, Peng Dehuai, He Long, Liu Bocheng, Li Jishen, Guo Moruo, Lin Feng, Liao Chengzhi, Yang Chengwu, Xu Guangping, Deng Tuo, Zheng Zhenduo, Wang Yeqiu, Wang Kunlun, Qi Yanming, Yang Yong, Wang Ping and other Party and state leaders and famous personages.

The Museum of Dingling Mausoleum was formally opened to the public in Sep. 1959. The main exhibits are cultural relics unearthed from the underground palace, which are added with excavation photos of the crypt, tables and models. They are classified into gold ware, porcelain, silks, tin grave-goods, the Emperor's and Empresses' crowns, belts and ornaments, etc. The furnishings of the crypt have all along been shown basically in their original form revealed in the excavation, while the funeral objects, since a later time, have been displayed in the Ling'en Hall of Changling Mausoleum, numbering 195 pieces/sets (including replicas). In April 1985, the museum began to be opened to foreign visitors. Up to the present, the Dingling underground palace has been opened to the public for more than 40 years. Every tourist who comes to Beijing wants to go to the sights. The ancient monument Dingling greets its visitors from all directions with its restored splendor.

Appendix: The Emperors Resting in the Ming Tombs at Beijing

Tomb Name	Emperor's Name	Reign Title	Temple Title	Date of Throne Ascending	Age at Throne Ascending	Years of Reign	Date of Death	Age at Death	Position in Lineage
Changling	Zhu Di	Yongle	Chengzu	4th year,Jianwen reign (1402)	43	22	22nd year,Yongle reign (1424)	65	Zhu Yuanzhang's 4th son
Xianling	Zhu Gaochi	Hongxi	Renzong	22nd year,Yongle reign (1424)	47	1	1st year,Hongxi reign (1425)	48	Zhu Di's 1st son
Jingling	Zhu Zhanji	Xuande	Xuan-zong	1st year,Hongxi reign (1425)	28	10	10th year,Xuande reign (1435)	38	Zhu Gaochi's 1st son
Yuling	Zhu Qizhen	Zheng-tong	Yingzong	10th year,Xuande reign (1435)	9	14	Falling in capture in 9th moon,14th year,Zhengtong reign		Zhu Zhanji's 1st son
Maoling	Zhu Jianshen	Chen-ghua	Xianzong	8th year,Tianshun reign (1464)	18	23	23rd year,Chenghua reign (1487)	41	Zhu Qizhen's 1st son
Tailing	Zhu Youtang	Hongzhi	Xiaozong	23rd year,Chenghua reign (1487)	18	18	18th year,Hongzhi reign (1505)	36	Zhu Jianshen's 3rd son
Kangling	Zhu Hou-zhao	Zhengde	Wuzong	18th year,Hongzhi reign (1505)	15	16	16th year,Zhengde reign (1521)	31	Zhu Youtang's 1st son
Yongling	Zhu Hou-cong	Jiajing	Shizong	16th year,Zhengde reign (1521)	15	45	45th year,Jiajing reign (1567)	60	Zhu Youtang's nephew
Zhaoling	Zhu Zaihou	Longq-ing	Muzong	45th year,Jiajing reign (1567)	30	6	6th year,Longqing reign (1572)	36	Zhu Houcong's 3rd son
Dingling	Zhu Yijun	Wanli	Shenzong	6th year,Longqing reign (1572)	10	48	48th year,Wanli reign (1620)	58	Zhu Zaihou's 3rd son
Qingling	Zhu Chan-gluo	Taichang	Guang-zong	48th year,Wanli reign (1620)	39	30 days	1st year,Taichang reign (1620)	39	Zhu Yijun's 1st son
Deling	Zhu Youjiao	Tianqi	Xizong	1st year,Taichang reign (1620)	16	7	7th year,Tianqi reign (1627)	23	Zhu Changluo's 1st son
Siling	Zhu Youjian	Chong-zhen	Sizong	7th year,Tianqi reign (1627)	18	17	17th year,Chongzhen reign (1644)	35	Zhu Changluo's 5th son